The Science of Living
With Friendship and Peace

By Dueep J Singh

Health Learning Series

Mendon Cottage Books

JD-Biz Publishing

Disclaimer

The information is this book is provided for informational purposes only. It is not intended to be used and medical advice or a substitute for proper medical treatment by a qualified health care provider. The information is believed to be accurate as presented based on research by the author.

The contents are the author's opinions and research and the Author or Publisher is not responsible for damages or harm caused by implementing techniques written in this publication.

The author or publisher is not responsible for the use or safety of any diet, procedure or treatment mentioned in this book. The author or publisher is not responsible for errors or omissions that may exist.

Warning

The Book is for informational purposes only and before taking on any diet, treatment or medical procedure it is recommended to consult with your primary care provider.

Our books are available at

1. Amazon.com

2. Barnes and Noble

3. Itunes

4. Kobo

5. Smashwords

6. Google Play Books

Table of Contents

Introduction

The Science of Living is a new way of life, in which you are going to live your life, learning from the examples and experience of the people around you. Life is for living, not just for existing. And this life is for living Emperor size, holding every moment precious, because once it is gone, it is lost in the mists of the past. So, our Science of Living series give you lots of information of how you can live life fully, and enjoy the action of living on this earth, at this moment.

This is the third book in the series. And this talks about living with friendship and peace. Peace is an ephemeral thing, which everybody wishes, but it is so elusive. For millenniums people have been seeking ways to gain peace among mankind, but that is only possible when they understand the meaning of friendship. And man is naturally and genetically inclined not to hold out his hand in friendship to another one not of his race, caste, Creed, area or religion, because of his upbringing, innate bias, genetic instinct, history, or anything else which makes him feel, "I do not want you as my friend."

I do not like thee Dr. Fell
Why this is so I cannot tell
But this I know fully well
I do not like thee Dr. Fell.

Charles Lamb said this more than two centuries ago, but thinking about this, anyone can understand why people do not like others instinctively. There is no logical rhyme or reason for this – like or dislike. But there is something which tells them that friendly relationships with that particular person is going to harm them or going to cause them emotional, physical, mental or spiritual trouble. And that is the reason why so many of us do not make friends at all.

This book is going to give you information on how you can cherish and nourish peace and friendship, and thus understand the basis of the Science of Living and living Emperor size.

The Pleasure of Lasting Friendships

How many of us have the time to enjoy some stolen moments with our friends in today's frenzied and frantic lifestyle?

The pleasure and joy of lasting friendships today are diminishing because of our hectic lifestyles. There was a time, when these friendships could be leisurely cultivated and preciously cherished for a lifetime. These friendships were the Damon and Pythias , David and Jonathan type of friendships, when one loved his fellow man like a brother and knew the value of a returned equally warm friendship. But alas, let us look at the friendships today. What we have are friendships which serve a purpose, which are useful and which accrue some direct or indirect benefit, with a time limit of anywhere between one week to two years. Also, we are so cynical, that the first instinct we have when somebody wishes to be friendly with us is, "what can or what will I gain out of this friendship?"and "what is he/she going to gain out of this friendship?" and "is it really worth my while to encourage this acquaintance and friendship?"

I am talking about practical reality. Take my example. Acquaintances and Fair weather friends I have had many and many, but my real friends are few. Many of these real friends are scattered to the winds or gathered to their fathers. Many of my friends call themselves my friends, because they need something *of or from* me. This can be advice, support, guidance, help or anything else which they find helpful in order to survive. I call myself their acquaintance, because I do not need them for any of these matters, yet. However, because I find they really need me, I consider myself their friend and help them. Because that is what friends are for. This is the saddest part of being an adult, the looking at another person in a practical and materialistic light.

Those long-term friends of our childhood and youth were made when all of us were innocent children and the idea of a friendship was not a selfish one, but more of innocent companionship among peers. We neither expected anything of them, nor did they expect anything of us except those magic moments when we laughed, sang, played, studied, and enjoyed each other's company together. These friendships were emotional and spiritual. That was really the age of innocence. Those friendships survived down the years, because we understood each other and we knew each other very well. We knew each other's weaknesses and strengths and accepted them. That was because we had accepted them as part and parcel of our and their identities and individual personalities. Those were the points which made us wish to be their friends and made them wish to be our friends. The company of our peers were shaping us into the adults we were going to be, by rubbing off our rough edges and corners and teaching us how we would conduct ourselves in the future.

Friendships of our childhood and youth may endure when you grow up, if we are lucky.

However, as one grew up, one found out that one made acquaintances, not friends. The moment an acquaintance outlived its utility, it was dumped in favor of better and more beneficial alliances.

Friendships have, in other words, become transactions measured in financial and materialistic terms. They rarely is any emotional or spiritual bonding involved, which is why it is easy to say goodbye and move on. That is why you find so many people breaking off "friendships," and then getting annoyed because the friend cannot see any justified rhyme or reason for you deciding not to keep up an acquaintance anymore. No wonder so many people get hurt, because there read more in friendships, than you were ever willing to give. But alas, this is the sad scenario of the twenty-first century. One of the standard excuses which are offered to justify a lack of genuine, meaningful friendship is lack of time. According to these fair weather friends, they spend so much of time in their offices, commuting from their home to their office and the increasing pressure of bringing up their children, ensuring care of family members, who require their attention and support, and also financial reasons. Well, these are not unjustifiable or unreasonable reasons. Everyone who is a responsible member of a family with its own demands is going to face this one time or the other in his life. However, all those who manage to enrich their lives by adding friends and making time out for them, will soon appreciate the value of these friendships.

Good friendships are the ideas stress relievers, and morale boosters. Best friendships are, of course, those which are made in different walks of life, so that you can go to each different age group for advice, for entertainment, for sheer enjoyment and for recreation, whenever you can. Many people do not try this idea and stick to just their own age group.

I remember as a child of class V, in a new school, going to play with children of class II and class III. They were so thrilled to have somebody older than they coming and playing with them. I enjoyed their company, because I found them much more agreeable and cheerful than my own classmates who were more worried about getting good marks, or looking for "friends", who could share peanut brittle with them during the lunch break. They had begun to learn the meaning of fair weather friendship. Also, my classmates had begun to grow up and had begun to mouth the prejudices of their elders, spoken out of the mouths of babes and sucklings.

Half of the time they did not know what they said, but were repeating something some elder person had said in their hearing. They were slowly and steadily imbibing the subconscious and insidious poison of prejudice, bias, intolerance and bigotry. This should not be the heritage of any child ever, in any society. On the other hand, the younger children just knew how to enjoy life without worrying about what someone else said, as long as they could run about in the sun and shout long, loud and clear.

The kiddies taught me some songs, I taught them some foolish games. In fact, those little babies taught me more in just one day than what I had learned staying with my own classmates and playing the same old boring games, for two long, tedious months.

When I came back to my class, at the end of the recess time, one of the supercilious know it all bullies in my class said to me, "listen, DJ, you are a newcomer in this school. Do you know the rules? You do not play with the younger children." I in all innocence, said, "who made these silly rules? Let me go ask the principal. He is funny if he stops us from making friends with other children in our school." She tried to hush me down. These were her own childish boundaries, to which she had bound our class. According to her, we stuck onto our own. And everybody believed her, because she was of a quarrelsome nature and they wanted to keep the peace.

Naturally, I told her, that I would do as I wished. If I wanted to make friends with anyone who wanted to be friends with me, they were welcome and more than welcome. Besides, she was a fat silly bore. She really did not know any interesting games, and she wanted her cronies around her all the time. I would not limit myself to silly rules, which had no logical, sensible or intelligent basis.

Of course, all this was spoken in the vocabulary of a child, asking this perpetual questions, – *Give me a reason why. Who says so? Let me ask someone else. If this is true, who made this rule? But first, you explain why this is so.*

She was extremely horrified at this candid appraisal by a newcomer, but she could not say anything to me because everybody had begun to ask the reason why. Well, the end result was that there was no question of artificial boundaries and artificial segregation in the school, once they found out that I wanted to be friends with the whole school, because within two years, we would be transferred out, and would never ever meet again. Believe me, within three months, the whole atmosphere of the school had changed and all of us 400 students knew each other, and there was no question of anyone keeping just to his class or classmates.

And that is what we need to do today. Ask the reason why. Why cannot we do that as adults? What are we scared of?

Even at that young age, I knew the type of human being my friend, the bully would grow up into. Intolerant of other people, just because she had been brought up like that. She would travel throughout the land, but would never make friends, because they were not her people . Or because they did not belong to the same social status or standing and background similar to hers. She would limit herself to just a narrow boundary imposed on her by her bound, narrow, limited imagination and perhaps bigoted elders.

Poor unfortunate child. She would never enjoy long-lasting and life and spirit enriching friendships from all over the world, like I and my family did, lo these many years.

And she, as an adult, has never asked herself why she has limited herself since childhood to such narrow boundaries.

What Do We Expect From Our Friends?

Life is for living with friends to share in moments of delight and joy.

I remember a hilarious description of a friend talking about another "friend". "Oh, I can always count upon S. Whenever I need a friend, I can count upon her to let me down." Now, after I finished laughing, because I knew S and I knew that she was a fair weather friend, I was a bit sad. How many real friends did S. have? Not many, because her acquaintances – I would not call them friends – had already understood that she was fickle, and she could not be trusted. Her acquaintances had already gained her measure. They would perhaps like her company for a short period of time, because she was young, cheerful, and attractive, but they would not trust her with anything serious or responsible or meaningful which made up an integral part of their own lives. What a loss to S. Her easily read qualities were not those what solid and true everlasting friendship requires.

Real Friendship requires an effort of support, solidarity, trust, faith, responsibility and belief.

When I analyzed this, I began to count the numbers of real friends, who I believed had the capacity to inspire all these points given above. And I was surprised to see that I could count just a few of them on my fingers. But those were friends who stuck closer than a brother. And that was because, they felt that they could rely on me for exactly these same points. And believe you me, this is a great responsibility to have on one's shoulders.

What does it take to be a friend?

Friendship demands nothing but sincerity, honesty, and trust

Since the willingness to maintain these friendships is marginally present in a group of people who intend to keep their friendship/alliance, last for a long time, they now have to take the most important step. friendship is going to dwindle away, if there is nobody to nourish and cherish it. People may say that absence makes the heart grow fonder, but that does not work in maintaining long-term friendships. If prolonged absence makes your friend wonder where you are, and what you are up to, because longtime no see no hear at means that your friendship is dwindling away. You will soon reach the stage of apathy and no action, and there you are, your ties of friendship will have faded away into memories. On the other hand, you should not intrude so much and so often in a friend's private life, or interfere with his own handling of some personal affairs, that you begin to grow into an inquisitive, interfering nuisance. Make it a point to take out the time and adjust your routines to meet occasionally. Interact with each other, socialize and be there in each others' hour of need.

A good friend is always there to comfort you and support you

A mature and rich friendship is going to flourish only when each person is familiar with the others' attitudes, behaviors, habits, and even strong and weak points. This will help them put things in perspective without misunderstanding or jumping to any wrong conclusions.

I remember one instance, when I had a group of colleagues getting together every third Saturday to spend the evening together. Most of our families, accepted the fact that we needed an occasional girls night outs, so that we could eat, drink, be merry and unwind. As going out to restaurants was very expensive, which decided to hold these get-togethers at our homes, turn wise. In a couple of months we recognized the fact that one of our friends belonged to an ultraconservative family.

Moments of friendship are precious; cherish them.

Their background made them unable initiative of too much partying, which they considered wasting money in futile pursuits. Once we got the message, we just volunteered among ourselves to have parties at our own homes rather than force our friend to host any sort of get together in her house. We did this quietly, without asking too many questions are expressing any overt sympathy are making any sort of snide comments about 17th-century familial or parental tyranny in the twenty-first century. Some things are unforgivable, and they are best left unspoken. Our friend was very grateful to us for our understanding and mature reasoning. A little bit of sense went into enrichening our friendship which has grown down the decades. Besides, she showed her gratefulness for our understanding by adding to the party fun with her own delicious home-cooked meals. In this way our friendship has lasted for such a long time, and also has continued to be the source of joy and strength to all of us.

Friendships Affecting Relationships At Home

Believe it or not, you may find some relationships at home, breaking up, because someone or the other misunderstands a friendship. In many cases, it is a case of jealousy, especially when there is a platonic friendship which has been going on for a long time between a man and a woman. It takes a very sensible man or a woman to accept the fact that his partner is just "simple friends" with someone of the opposite sex. In Asia, of course, this is going to lead to plenty of family dissension, and relationships getting better with the ultimatums of "choose me, or choose her/him," being bandied about freely in the air. Also, it takes a very mature man – even in the West – to accept the fact that his very attractive wife has a male colleague who shares portions of her professional life with her. Until he is he is reassured that he is the one best beloved, over all, and the other man is just a colleague, he is always going to have this sneaking suspicion whether the friendship was not something warmer in the past, or it is not going to turn into something warmer in the future.

Believe it or not, a majority of men and women out there go into marriage with the thought that there is a possibility that their partner is going to cheat on them. That is why they keep testing out their partners in order to catch them out in a lie or a falsehood. This suspicion is innate, and natural. But the sad thing is that many times beautiful relationships are destroyed, because of the suspicious nature of one of the partners, who cannot believe the fact that any sort of friendship is limited to just a friendship and nothing more. That is because they are analyzing the psyche of their partners, according to their own concept of friendship and more than friendship. If they had friends, and that friendship grew into something warmer like an affair, before they married the women/man of their choice there are always going to think, "if that happened with me, why should not it happened to her/him." Many partners then decide to break long-term friendships, in order to keep peace in the home.

Could it be possible that…? Should I ask him about…? Is he…? Why did he…?

Now if we take the example of our friend and how our understanding managed to prevent any sort of friction in her home, that is because we had the sense and compassion enough to understand the circumstances in her house. She could have protested against and resented the old-fashioned ideas of the family into which she had married. This would have caused unnecessary friction and bitterness between her husband and her.

In this case, we as friends provided the ideal cushion to the loving relationship of a happily married couple. Her husband knows that his wife goes out every third Saturday to one of her old friends'house, with plenty of delicious cooked dishes. He used to accompany her, being too shy to join in the festivities, but when he found out that all the males had teamed out on a boys night out, he decided to join them! So now there are twelve families who have enriched their lives, with interaction between each other, just starting with a group of twelve women working together, deciding to make up a friendly team.

Now this is what friendship should be all about, companionship, fun, relaxation, time to unwind, so that your sense of balance is restored and thus everyone can cope with their high pressure jobs, problems in parenting, problems with family members and other natural elements of a human being's social, emotional, mental, financial and personal life.

You need to be conscious of the fact that it takes very little to ruin a long-standing relationship, however strong and serious it may be. That is why many people work constantly at keeping their friendships intact and make sure that they always added good value and depth to what they share with their friends.

Here are some golden rules about keeping those friendships everlasting.

The Golden Rules about Friendship

Golden Principle Number One – No Loose Talk

Many people think that gossip is the spice of life!

Believe it or not, *Thou Shall Not Bear False Witness* is a Commandment which plays a very important role in keeping your friendship everlastingly strong. Look at the meaning of these words. How many times have you borne against your neighbor, or any of your friends? Never, you say indignantly, you never had an opportunity to say anything false against them in court or anywhere else. Uh-huh! Think very carefully. How many times have you passed on a piece of gossip, which was too spicy to keep to yourself to somebody else? It is possible you just exaggerated a wee bit to make it more spicier. After all, XYZ lunching out with J.'s husband – you know that it was a business meeting, but you wanted to just get things moving – is something that you need to share with everybody in the office and in the vicinity, especially with J. How many of us have been prompted out of sheer mischief to do just this. Believe it or not, I know a lot of people, who positively enjoy stirring up things, and then looking as innocent as a newborn lamb when trouble and strife follows. They seem to be in some sort of inner satisfaction and feel some sort of triumph that they are the instigators of such problems just with their carelessly spoken word into the ears of a receptive immature blabbermouth. Loose talking is one of the things a good friend never indulges in, not even in jest.

 If you know any of your friends who indulges in such behavior, just shun his company. If he can tell stories about R. in your presence, it is possible that he is telling R. stories about you, without fail. And if you were amused at the exaggerations in that story, knowing them fully well to be untrue, but listening to them, because they were so spicy, think about the tale he is going to tell R about you, with extra embellishments and exaggerations. And that means be very cautious in the company of such dangerous acquaintances.

 Also, if you have a friend who comes to you and whines about twenty people and how miserable they are making them, every day, you may want to ask him, if he is not the problem, and he is the reason why those twenty people are miserable. This sort of clear-sightedness comes only with experience and the ability to think clearly. Making fun of a friend, especially in his/her absence is something you should never do because it could cause a lot of hurt and pain to the person concerned. Because you can be certain that there is some altruistic human in that listening circle who is going to go straight to that friend and under a sweetly smiling garb of "I think you should know, after all, I am your well wisher," repeat your words, along with some words from their own imagination. That is that. A friendship has been broken, because you hurt your friend just because you wanted to amuse some other people in a moment of euphoria or lightheartedness.

Straightforward, sincere, and honest communication between friends instead of gossiping behind the back strengthens a friendship.

If you have something to say something about someone, always express your concern to the person directly, rather than indulge in a long winded conversation behind that person's back. There are times when a well-meaning dialogue can be misconstrued and the context changed, creating misunderstandings and destroying relationships.

Criticizing each other, discussing private details and gossiping over trivial things may be very amusing as children or as youths, because that is the time when we are trying out our social wings. We are looking at the limitations to which we are bound by society, tradition, upbringing, financial background and other matters, which we consider to be of extreme importance to us. On the other hand, if we still continue this sort of behavior, when we are adults, we are going to be deemed to be pests, nuisances, and definitely not good friend material. We are going to be labeled great big Bores, harping on one everlasting theme by other people. And soon we are going to find ourselves with just one friend/enemy – and he can be seen when we look at ourselves in the mirror.

So if you find somebody trying to rope you into such a conversation, you can either politely get up and move away on some paltry excuse, and if that is not possible, you can pretend to be stoned deaf or noncommittal. Remember the moment you leave the group that cynical person is going to say something on the lines of Connie Russo speaking about Angela DeMarco, who has just turned down her overture of friendship in Married To The Mob- "That snooty b...., she thinks..." This is the common reaction of a person, who is faced with somebody who does not accept an overture of friendship. But why would you want to be friends with the person who just wants to be friends with you because of selfish reasons?

This sort of noncommittal behavior will make all your friends know that you are extremely trustworthy and you are not going to indulge in whose stock of any sort. Also, you live by certain values and principles and that is why you are ideal friend material. They can share secrets, open their heart, cry on your shoulder and be sure that all this would not be broadcasted out in the world or posted on Facebook. They understand that you know what to say and how much to say in front of others. This shows that you are tactful, discrete and you behave with maturity, especially where it matters most. That will make you very much in demand as a trusted and very valuable cherished friend.

Golden Principle Number Two – Friends taking advantage?

Why do nations get into uneasy alliances, with one nation accruing all the benefits, and the other nation just getting a feeling that it has a mighty power behind it to support it? This is the matter of nations. The same thing works in the matter of individual friends. Your friends want your support. They are going to be friendly with you only when they know that they are going to gain emotionally, spiritually and mentally from you. Financial gain and the motive of friendship based on financial give-and-take is more of an acquaintance because it is being done through purely selfish and unaltruistic motives.

Once I asked a colleague of mine, why she was very choosy about the friends she made. Her answer was, "well, DJ, the problem is that most of the friends that I make have some ulterior motive. Also, I keep thinking about what they want from me, when I set out to make friends. Once I can persuade my mind, that they do not intend to demand anything of me, spiritually, emotionally, mentally, financially or even physically, I can then proceed with making friends with them." Alas, this is the mental outlook of a majority of us.

Throughout our lives, many of us have noticed that there are friends, who are going to take advantage of us sometime or the other until it may grow to be a wearisome burden. That is why, here is the second Golden principle –

use your own judgment. Learn how to say no. And mean it when you say no. Then somebody needs help, you need to look at the situation carefully. Is it a genuine case? Go ahead, help them, if you are in the condition to do so. If you have pressing commitments, which take on top priority, express your inability to help them. A little bit of frankness right now goes a long way in preventing future strains in your friendship.

I remember a colleague S. who strained the limits to our friendships by being broke by the fifteenth of the month, every month. For one or two months, we gave her loans of small amounts of money – which she promptly returned on payday, I will give her that – but when we got together, and found that she had been borrowing money from all of us, every month for the past three months, without fail, we decided to put our foot down. Next time she came to me, asking for a small loan to tide her over, I said, "hey, I am sorry, I cannot give you any money, but we can ask R., N., and K., if they have any money to loan you." And I called them over. S. was in squirming mode, when N. [who sees himself as a future Oscar winner, but is a very amusing ham actor,] did a double take, widened his gray eyes eyes very wide and said, "What, has she been borrowing money from you too,guys? I thought I was the only one and I tided her over because she needed it. What have you been doing with all the money I lent you, these three months,S?" Later we found out that her sob story was totally imaginary. She wanted to buy the latest Gucchi bags and brand designer outfits as they came into the market, every month, and had been doing so for the past three months.

This was an acquaintanceship, we dropped like a hot potato.

Fool me once, shame on you, fool me twice, shame on me.

It took a little bit of experience and a little bit of communication which helped us from carrying a parasite on our backs, because soon, she would be a whiner, to whom we could not say no, just because we were too polite to do so and we did not like her bursting into tears or putting on the emotional waterworks. That is what she did with the men. With us, it was a long sob story with an aging and ailing relative who needed medical aid.

Shakespeare had it down pat, "neither a borrower nor a lender be." In fact, this piece of wisdom was told to me by an old wise graybeard, "If you want to get rid of a friend, who is very tiresome, lend him a large amount of money. Then ask for the money, whenever you meet him. You will have lost the money, but you will also have the pleasure of his absence from your vicinity."

So, learn to say no. If you do not want to lend your car to a friend who is known to be rough with his driving and maintenance, say no very clearly. It is much better to have him pouting and sulking rather than you agreeing and then holding it against the other person for a life time, just because you did not have the courage to speak out.

True friends are going to understand and respect your decisions. Those who are not, are going to move away from you, to other people who are more susceptible and vulnerable to their parasitical and selfish personalities. This genuineness of communication and sincerity is going to make people very secure of your friendship. Most of your friends are going to go out of their way to reciprocate your actions with sincere actions of their own if necessary or when needed.

The way you conduct yourself with your friends should make them feel at ease with you. Friendships, based on intimidation, fear, jealousy, and envy are never going to succeed. That is because one of your friends is not enjoying your company as a friend, but is spending his time saying mentally, "Gr-r-r—there go, my heart's abhorrence!"[1] whenever he is in your presence. Unfortunately, envy, and jealousy is the reason why so many friendships break up. That is because you are competing subconsciously against somebody else, who you believe to be superior to you in brains, and ability, aptitude, financial status, or anything else. That is why, you spend most of your time trying to compete with him, consciously or subconsciously and thus, you live your life in a never-ending competing rat race.

There is no end to an unhealthy competition. A sensible person is not going to lose sleep over the fact that a friend of your group has just bought a new car, while you are still zipping around in your tiny old roadster. If you are genuinely happy when others are successful in their professional, personal or social life, without an iota of envy or resentment, your friends are going to appreciate you for what you are and for your friendship.

There is no duplicity or double standard in a good friends' behavior. Also, they do not suffer from any complexes – superiority or inferiority! They are what they are and they expect others to accept them that way. There is no hypocrisy or artificiality in them. They do not try to upstage any of their friends or try to compete with them. This is a natural and spontaneous friendship which they offer to the people around them.

While you being human, you may envy the lifestyle, the looks, the success or the confidence of your friends around you, you are not going to say anything derogatory or try to run them down in order to boost your own ego. This is a difficult golden rule to follow, but it helps in the long run. It

---

[1] Robert Browning – Soliloquy of the Spanish Cloister – read In Appendix about Brother Lawrence and one of his fellow monks.

also makes sure that you do not suffer from envy and jealousy, and also adds to your peace of mind and spiritual growth.

If you are comfortable with what you are and what you have, it is this quiet confidence in yourself and acceptance as well as nonjudgmental attitude towards others which are going to make others feel secure in your friendship.

Misunderstandings Among Friends

Open lines of communication prevent misunderstandings between friends

The major basis of a relationship, as well as the friendship is clear communication. There is no place for pride or an inflated ego in a relationship. It may often happen that you may find situations or matters escalating in an uncomfortable and ugly manner, due to some implied, or apparent action or statement. A sensible person is always going to tackle the issue head first. How many times do you find yourself too cowardly to tackle an issue, and hoping against hope that it is going to go away if you ignore it? We have done this many times in our personal and professional lives. Those issues are going to remain there and one fine day, they are going to be staring at us, the moment we wake up, with absolutely no intention of leaving until they have been solved. So here are some points which you need to practice when you are tackling an issue of a misunderstanding among friends. First find out what has hurt or upset the other person. Are you to blame for the misunderstanding? Did you do or say something which had triggered off the ill feelings? If you are in any way responsible, do not hesitate in a sincere and genuine apology if not, clear the air by putting forth your point of view. Do not let matters rest because that is only going to aggravate matters, and cause them to escalate.

This reminds me of an incident. I knew of a friend K. who was considered to be very trustworthy. She gave good advice to all of us and especially to a friend A. who needed it very often. In fact, A. spent a lot of time asking K's advice, and implementing it. Why not take advantage of experience when it is there. One fine day, we noticed that A. had begun to avoid K. K. did not bother about that much, until she spoke to A. and asked her if she had hurt her in some way or had inadvertently done or said something to upset her? "I asked you, just for a small favor, for months ago, because I thought you my friend. Instead, you could not care less about the favor, so I decided that you really did not care."

All of us got to know the story, during the explanations. A. had a brother who needed a recommendation from someone he knew, in order to get a good job. K. had provided to the recommendation and handed it over to A.'s secretary, to pass on to A. The secretary had left the organization within the week, and without passing on the recommendation to A. The brother did not get that job because his employers did not receive the recommendation. And here was K thinking that he had already received the job, but had not asked A. about her brother's success or failure. In the same manner, A. was very disappointed at what she thought was K's callous attitude and indifference towards a small requests for a recommendation.

Had K not confronted it, she would probably have lost a rich friendship in bitterness, but since she did, she got the chance to explain, and present her side of the story in detail. Both of them thrashed it out, with all of us umpiring and applauding, and now we are all back to being the good friends, we are.

So just see, a little word spoken at the right time could have saved four months of bitterness. Why do we not speak it? That is because we could not be bothered. Also, the fear of hearing something unpleasant, which could point at our own inadequacy or inability often prevents us from confronting issues and talking about them in a forthright manner.

However, if you do not want to lose the friendship, and you know that you are confident enough to handle a situation, and you are prepared to face possibly unpleasant issues in a forthright manner, well, you are someone brave.

But that is only if you have the courage and the power to look inwards and see if you have indeed been wrong. Most of us do not accept the fact that we may be wrong somewhere. We would rather blame the other person and let matters go from there. We do not want to be told that we are wrong, which is why the avoid taking up issues up front. We continue sugarcoating reality until things get really bad, and the damage becomes irreversible. That is the defense mechanism put up by our brains to save us from mental and emotional turmoil and pain. The mind immediately is going to take the line of least resistance. So that is the stage when personal ties snap and it becomes very difficult to turn the clock back.

Social Life And Personal Life

Priorities of our hectic lifestyle have shifted in such a way that friendships, – especially those which one had in school or at work, – somehow do not seem to fit into one's personal life as we grow older. One loses touch with one's friends and gets out of circulation because something else is taking top priority in our lives.

Another common thing which is responsible for soaring friendships is the lack of appreciation from one of the spouses.

Give me patience! How on earth does he expect me to feed all his good for nothing lazy lumps of friends, which he invited over for the weekend? Men are so heedless…

I have a couple of friends, J and Kay. J is extrovertish , outgoing and comes from a blue-collar, working-class man background. His wife, Kay can be considered to be from the right side of the tracks with a white lace curtain Bostonian blueblood background. We were very surprised when these two people from such disproportionate backgrounds decided to get married, but they were the ideal made for each other couple, because both were sensible, intelligent and adaptive, as long as their families kept out of their personal lives. They have been happily married for the past twelve years, which is rather amazing taking into view the amount of pressure both of them have to face, trying to adapt to each other's lifestyles and families.

J is very sensible in the manner, that he stopped going to any of his wife's posh family get-togethers, because he did not want her to feel uncomfortable with his presence. He knew that that would subconsciously have an effect on her and their happy family life. All of us admire him a lot for that.

Nevertheless, ten years down the line, J does not have any friends. The reason – they think that Kay does not approve of them, or that she looks down on them.

It did not occur to J's friends that they could still have kept up their friendship with him, without putting Kay to the trouble of enduring people she supposedly did not fancy. Also, J, took this breaking off of ties with his erstwhile friends as a direct insult to himself, his ego, his pride and also to Kay, who unknowingly was the unconscious reason for this breaking of fast and past friendships.

What a pity. A little bit of talking mano-a- mano would have cleared up things wonderfully well for J, and he would not be friendless, these past five years.

So remember, the support of your friends is a social lifeline as well as a source of sustenance, emotionally, mentally, socially, and spiritually.

Keeping the friends you have, and cherishing this friendship is thus one of the top priorities of a person who understands The Science of Living.

Peace Among Mankind

This is of course the dearest wish of all mankind, through millenniums, but we know that it is not possible. But it is such a good thing to look forward. Why is there no peace in the hearts and souls of men? Women, of course, have been suffering in silence through the ages as their men go off to war. I remember an instant, when a politician friend of mine came back from a meeting really het up against her male colleagues. "Talk, talk, talk, that is what they do. Actually, they should leave these talking processes to us women, who know exactly all about peacemaking and friendship. Let somebody come up with some practical and according to them, reasonable reason why this peace treaty should not be negotiated, and we are going to see trouble in this area for the next couple of years more. On the other hand, let some women from our side, and some women from their side get together and decide how peace talks should be negotiated with our sons and husbands not going off to war. And see what we can do."

I am ashamed to say I laughed. Not going to happen. That is because people making decisions go in for practical and logical decisions, according to them, and not emotional decisions which may be more beneficial in the long run. But who looks for benefit, when one is talking about short-term gains to a limited number of individuals in the form of financial power, and political power and the rest of the world can go and fight, suffer and die all in the name of patriotism.

This is the age of Aquarius. This should be the century of peace. But why is man not willing to tolerate his fellow man?

Maybe some of the questions can be answered in this poem which I wrote about two decades ago when I was in my 20s, idealistic, and believed that mankind could live in peace and harmony. John Lennon sang that in the 60s, in *Imagine* and so did Roger Whittaker in *I do not believe in if anymore*. We may feel bitter and cynical today, but hope is everlasting.

Here is Eve's song. It was originally written in French by me, and this is the English translation of friendship and strife.

Eve's Song.

He was finding His Universe quite serene.

The stars were singing in their spheres. And the Spheres,

Were swaying to their own rhythm.

To their own *Te Diem.*

In their praise of Him.

The is the time for Everything, the moment, the season.

A method to his Mirth, some rhyme and reason.

Which made him pick up a clod of clay and fashion it into a human.

He shall exult in my Creations; he shall sing my praises forever.

And while he created Eve, he heard,

The very first clod say his very first word

to his brother clod of Clay.

No, my brother no, my brother, you shall not say *Allah Hu*!

To praise Him; he is for ever *Mon Dieu*!

And the first blow was struck in His Name.

And He spoke, Oh my, what have I wrought?

And Eve smiled sadly and spoke.

Forgive them My Father, for they do not know what they say,

And worse still... They know not what they do!

No my brother, I do not like your hue.

No my brother, I do not like You.

Since that date,

Eve has watched quietly as her Adam,

Reduces his Abel's Heritage to ashes and dust

All in the name of preserving and protecting it.

Or in the adding of his Abel's land and boundaries.

And all this is done in His name or for His Sake for ages, eons and millenniums,

It is time for Eve to get up today,

And say, enough, my Man!

Stop cutting your brother man into pieces while you are cutting up our peace!

Eve has the Power to show the true strength which lies in gentleness.

Because He gave her the mother's the wife's, the sister's, the daughter's gentleness of true strength,

To bear her Crosses at all her Calvarys.

To put out her hand across the sea

in friendship and amity

For the sake of her children.

When her Adam went off to war...

Now, this is talking about friendship, peace and amity on a global scale. This is, sadly, pipe dream in this day and age, though we live in hope. Nevertheless, friendships are the lifeline in modern times, when we hope that we have enough of good friends who can give us the right physical as his sense, necessary emotional support, and even in some cases the right spiritual insights, required to help us get through life.

Conclusion

Friendships today require a lot of investment in terms of time, effort, money and patience, but those who have made that investment have realized that they have made a profitable long-term lifelong deal, which is spiritually, emotionally and mentally satisfying the idea is not to have hordes of friends, just having two or three families with whom one can meet and interact can provide just the right balance.

Friends act as your moral guardians too. they can be taken into confidence in intensely private matters and you can expect them to give you the best advice, depending on their experience and knowledge. Friends are there to support you, help you take care of your health, self-esteem, and also to help in the bonding of family and society.

Friendships, more than anything else, requires sensitivity, empathy, and the ability to step beyond one's own boundaries. And once we do that, we find ourselves being rewarded with so much more love and compassion. So, now that you know all about the golden rules of friendship, you can understand how integral it is In the Science of Living.

May you have many good friends and may all of them think that you are a good friend too!

Author Bio

Dueep Jyot Singh is a Management and IT Professional who managed to gather Postgraduate qualifications in Management and English and Degrees in Science, French and Education while pursuing different enjoyable career options like being an hospital administrator, IT,SEO and HRD Database Manager/ trainer, movie scriptwriter, theatre artiste and public speaker, lecturer in French, Marketing and Advertising, ex-Editor of Hearts On Fire (now known as Solctice) Books Missouri USA, advice columnist and cartoonist, publisher and Aviation School trainer, ex- moderator on Medico.in, banker, student councilor ,travelogue writer … among other things! One fine morning, she decided that she had enough of killing herself by Degrees and went back to her first love -- writing. It's more enjoyable! She already has 48 published academic and 14 fiction- in- different- genre books under her belt.

When she is not designing websites or making Graphic design illustrations for clients who want Walt Disney, Norman Rockwell , JJ Grandville or Hed Kandy type illustrations, she is busy browsing in old bookshops for antique books,-she has a mouthwatering collection of priceless First editions and rare books…including R.L. Stevenson, O.Henry, Dornford Yates, Maurice Walsh, C.N.Williamson, and the crown of her collection- Dickens "The Old Curiosity Shop," and so on… Just call her "Renaissance Woman" - collecting herbal remedies, making one of a kind creations in Irish Crochet and Aran knitting, acting like Universal Helping Hand/Agony Aunt, or escaping to her dear mountains for a bit of exploring, collecting herbs and plants , trekking, and rappelling.

Check out some of the other JD-Biz Publishing books

Download Free Books!

http://MendonCottageBooks.com

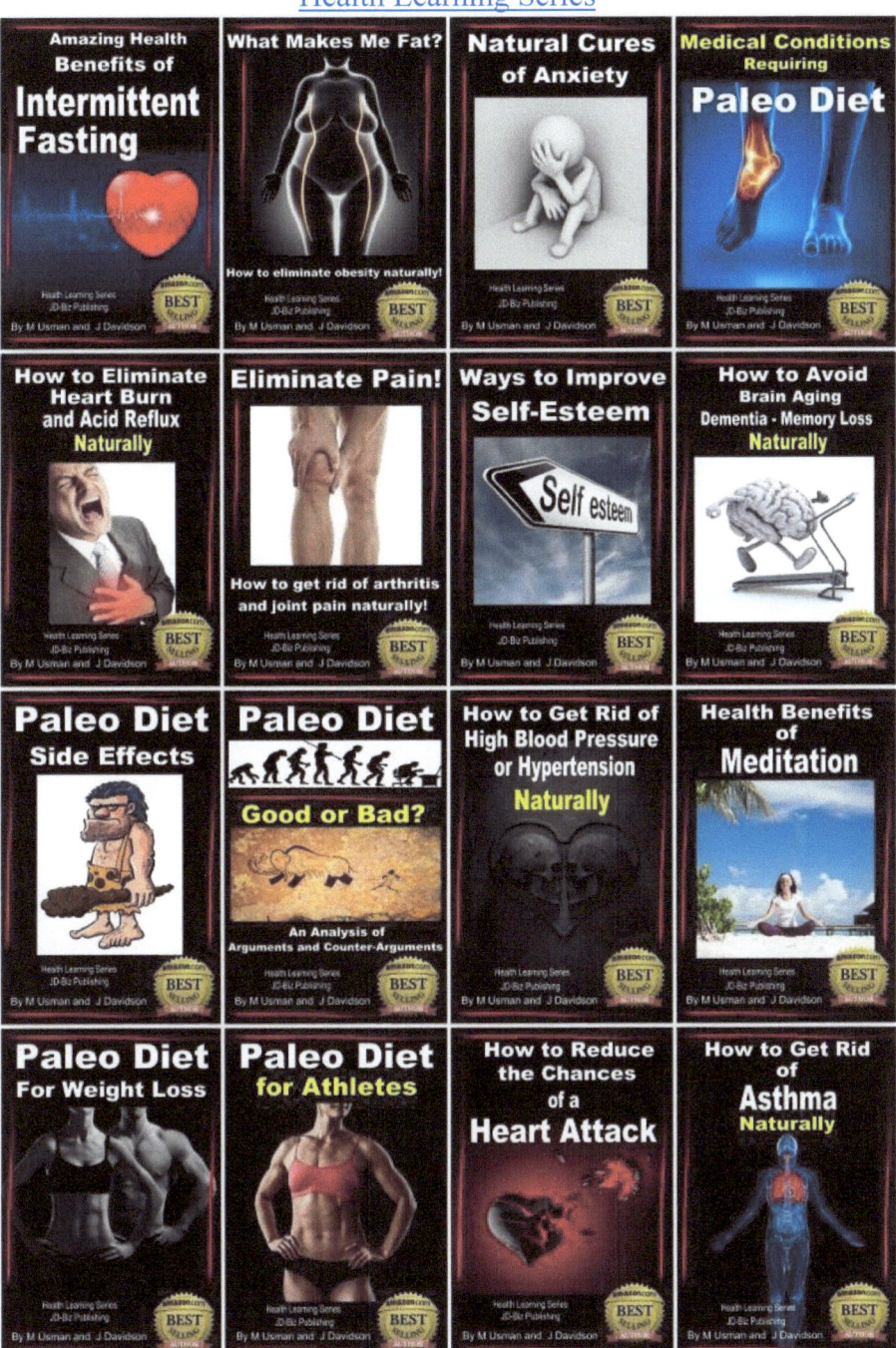

How to Build and Plan Books

Entrepreneur Book Series

Our books are available at

1. Amazon.com
2. Barnes and Noble
3. Itunes
4. Kobo
5. Smashwords
6. Google Play Books

Download Free Books!

http://MendonCottageBooks.com

Publisher

JD-Biz Corp

P O Box 374

Mendon, Utah 84325

http://www.jd-biz.com/

Mendon Cottage Books

P O Box 374, Mendon Utah 84325

www.ingramcontent.com/pod-product-compliance
Lightning Source LLC
Chambersburg PA
CBHW050831290526
45792CB00001B/347